Retail assistants do lots of different jobs in a shop. They may be involved with restocking, cleaning and refunding.

In some shops, retail assistants might greet you at the door. They may even offer to help you find what you are looking for.

Can you sort these words into two groups?
One group has e as in **end**.
One group has e as in **email**.

sequin

vegan

egg

she

Venus

pet

bell

check

Do you ever think about the people who help you when you shop? These are retail assistants.

Retail

Level 7 – Turquoise

Helpful Hints for Reading at Home

The graphemes (written letters) and phonemes (units of sound) used throughout this series are aligned with Letters and Sounds. This offers a consistent approach to learning, whether reading at home or in the classroom.

HERE IS A LIST OF PHONEMES FOR THIS PHASE OF LEARNING. AN EXAMPLE OF THE PRONUNCIATION CAN BE FOUND IN BRACKETS.

Phase 5			
ay (day)	ou (out)	ie (tie)	ea (eat)
oy (boy)	ir (girl)	ue (blue)	aw (saw)
wh (when)	ph (photo)	ew (new)	oe (toe)
au (Paul)	a_e (make)	e_e (these)	i_e (like)
o_e (home)	u_e (rule, cube)		

Phase 5 Alternative Pronunciations of Graphemes			
a (hat, what)	e (bed, she)	i (fin, find)	o (hot, so, other)
u (but, unit)	c (cat, cent)	g (got, giant)	ow (cow, blow)
ie (tied, field)	ea (eat, bread)	er (farmer, herb)	ch (chin, school, chef)
y (yes, by, very)	ou (out, shoulder, could, you)		

HERE ARE SOME WORDS WHICH YOUR CHILD MAY FIND TRICKY.

Phase 5 Tricky Words			
oh	their	people	Mr
Mrs	looked	called	asked
could			

TOP TIPS FOR HELPING YOUR CHILD TO READ:

- Allow children time to break down unfamiliar words into units of sound and then encourage children to string these sounds together to create the word.
- Encourage your child to point out any focus phonics when they are used.
- Read through the book more than once to grow confidence.
- Ask simple questions about the text to assess understanding.
- Encourage children to use illustrations as prompts.

This book focuses on /e/ and the alternative pronunciations of its grapheme. It is a Turquoise level 7 book band.

As they are in the shop from morning to evening, they can point you the right way. They can tell you the exact shelf that you need.

When the products on a shelf run out, the assistants will restock them. They check that there are equal amounts of stock on each shelf.

They have to make sure that each thing is not out of date and has the right price on it.

Sometimes, retail assistants need to deal with problems such as spills and breaks. They help keep the shop clean when it is needed.

When people are finished with their shopping, they bring it all to the till. Here, retail assistants scan them in and take payment for them.

If a customer brings something back to the shop for a refund, a retail assistant can help them.

They will check that all the details are correct so that they can repay the person the right amount. The refunded items can be resold if there are no problems with them.

Until now, you may not have realised just how much retail assistants do in their job.

Next time someone helps you while you are shopping, make sure to thank them.

©2023 **BookLife Publishing Ltd.**
King's Lynn, Norfolk, PE30 4LS, UK

ISBN 978-1-80505-105-3

All rights reserved. Printed in China.
A catalogue record for this book is available from the British Library.

Retail
Written by Charis Mather
Designed by Lucy Otter

An Introduction to BookLife Readers...

Our Readers have been specifically created in line with the London Institute of Education's approach to book banding and are phonetically decodable and ordered to support each phase of the Letters and Sounds document.

Each book has been created to provide the best possible reading and learning experience. Our aim is to share our love of books with children, providing both emerging readers and prolific page-turners with beautiful books that are guaranteed to provoke interest and learning, regardless of ability.

BOOK BAND GRADED using the Institute of Education's approach to levelling.

PHONETICALLY DECODABLE supporting each phase of Letters and Sounds.

EXERCISES AND QUESTIONS to offer reinforcement and to ascertain comprehension.

CLEAR DESIGN to inspire and provoke engagement, providing the reader with clear visual representations of each non-fiction topic.

AUTHOR INSIGHT:
CHARIS MATHER

Charis Mather is a children's author at BookLife Publishing who has a love for reading and writing. Her studies in linguistics and experiences working with young readers have given her a knack for writing material that suits a range of ages and skill levels. Charis is passionate about producing books that emphasise the fun in reading and is convinced that no matter how much you already know, there is always something new to learn.

This book focuses on /e/ and the alternative pronunciations of its grapheme. It is a Turquoise level 7 book band.

Image Credits Images are courtesy of Shutterstock.com. With thanks to Getty Images, Thinkstock Photo and iStockphoto. Cover – 9nong, Flat_Enot, GoodStudio, Juan Pablo Olaya Celis, Little_Monster_2070. 4–5 – Stokkete, XiXinXing. 6–7 – Odua Images, Tyler Olson. 8–9 – FTiare, wavebreakmedia. 10–11 – Dmitry Kalinovsky, sirtravelalot. 12–13 – Marc Calleja, Odua Images. 14–15 – stockfour, Tyler Olson.